Country Kitchen Collection

Kitchen Garden

Camille Pissarro (1830-1903) Plum Trees in Bloom

Country Kitchen Collection

Kitchen Garden

Anna Nicholas

Sir Luke Fildes (1844-1927) *Peeling Potatoes*

Grange BOOKS

ACKNOWLEDGEMENTS
All pictures by courtesy of The Bridgeman Art Library

Peeling Apples by John Edward Cobbett (1815-1899) Harrogate Museums and Art Gallery, North Yorkshire/ Bridgeman Art Library, London. The Onion Boy, 1902 by Stanhope Alexander Forbes (1857-1947) Phillips, The Fine Art Auctioneers/London Bridgeman Art Library, London. Still Life with Tomatoes and Cucumbers by Luis Menendez or Melendez (1716-1780) Prado, Madrid/Bridgeman Art Library, London. Washing the Vegetables by Frederick Richard Pickersgill (1820-1900) Phillips, The Fine Art Auctioneers, London/Bridgeman Art Library, London. Shelling Peas, published in 'Lasst Licht Hinin' ('Let in More Light'), 1909 by Carl Larsson (1853-1919) Stapleton Collection /Bridgeman Art Library, London. Market Garden at Chelsea by George Barret the Younger (1767-1842) Victoria and Albert Museum, London /Bridgeman Art Library, London. La Rue des Abbesses by Maximilien Luce (1858-1941) Petit Palais, Geneva/ Bridgeman Art Library, London. The Market at Marseilles, 1905 by Raoul Dufy (1877-1953) Petit Palais, Geneva/DACS 1996/ Bridgeman Art Library, London. Garden in Grez, 1884 by Karl Fredrick Nordstrom (1855-1923) Goteborgs Konstmuseum, Sweden/Bridgeman Art Library, London. The Cabbage Slopes, Pontoise, 1882 by Camille Pissarro (1830-1903) Private Collection/Bridgeman Art Library, London. Vegetable Garden at the Hermitage, Pontoise, 1879 by Camille Pissarro (1830-1903) Musée d'Orsay, Paris /Bridgeman Art Library, London. The Vegetable Seller by Joachim Beuckelaer or Bueckelaer (c.1530-1573) Musée des Beaux-Arts, Valenciennes /Bridgeman Art Library, London/Giraudon. The Allotment Garden by Sir George Clausen (1852-1944) The Fine Art Society, London/Bridgeman Art Library, London. A Cottage Garden by Myles Birket Foster (1825-1899) The British Museum/Bridgeman Art Library, London. At the Dose Venier by Walter Frederick Roofe Tyndale (1856-1943) Chris Beetles Ltd., London/Bridgeman Art Library, London. The Greengrocer, 1731 by Willem van Mieris (1662-1747) Wallace Collection/Bridgeman Art Library, London. Still Life by Michelangelo Merisi da Caravaggio (1573-1610) Private Collection/Bridgeman Art Library, London. The Potato Harvest by Ernest Masson (19th century) Musée de Roubaix, France/Bridgeman Art Library, London/ Giraudon. Provençal Cookery by Antoine Raspal (1738-1811) Musée Réattu, Arles/Bridgeman Art Library, London/Giraudon. Sorting Garlic by JohnBulloch Souter (1890-1972) City of Edinburgh Museums and Art Galleries/Bridgeman Art Library, London. Dolly by Sir Luke Fildes (1844-1927) Warrington Museum and Art Gallery), Lancs./Bridgeman Art Library, London. Vegetable Market by Lucas van Valkenborch (c.1535-1597) Kunsthistorisches Museum, Vienna/Bridgeman Art Library, London. The Greengrocer (fresco), Italian School (15th century) Castle of Issogne or Challant Castle, Piedmont/Bridgeman Art Library, London. A Girl in a Garden by the Sea by Henry Maynell Rheam (1859-1920) Whitford & Hughes, London/Bridgeman Art Library, London. Miss Lydiard's Stall, Bath by Walter Frederick Roofe Tyndale (1856-1943) Chris Beetles Ltd., London/Bridgeman Art Library, London. The Square in Front of Les Halles by Victor Gabriel Gilbert (1847-1933) Musée des Beaux-Arts, Le Havre /Bridgeman Art Library, London. Gardening by Stanley Spencer (1891-1959) Private Collection/Estate of Stanley Spencer 1996. All rights reserved DACS/Bridgeman Art Library, London. Peeling Potatoes by Sir Luke Fildes (1944-1927) Christopher Wood Gallery, London/Bridgeman Art Library, London. An Amateur by Frederick Walker 1840-1875) British Museum, London/ Bridgeman Art Library, London. Plum Trees in Flower by Camille Pissarro (1830-1903) Christie's, London/Bridgeman Art Library, London. Cottages at Broadway by Ernest Albert Chadwick (1876-1956) Fine-Lines (Fine Art), Warwickshire/Bridgeman Art Library, London.

The Publishers have made every effort to trace the copyright holders of material reproduced within this compilation. If, however, they have inadvertantly made any error they would be grateful for notification.

Published in 1996
by Grange Books
An imprint of Grange Books Plc.
The Grange
Grange Yard
London SE1 3AG

ISBN 1 85627 739 9

Printed in China

This book is not intended to be an in-depth look at the technique of cooking: there are a myriad of books which do just this and which go into the nuances of producing many of the dishes described in this volume, most of which have been around for a very long time and exist in many variations even across national boundaries. It is a celebration of food in its wider sense; as an important part of the development of civilized behaviour in which society is bonded together in the acts of eating, discussing and depicting food which is, after all, a prime necessity for our continued existence.

Frederick Walker (1840-1875) *An Amateur*

Foreword

At this moment in time, there appears to be an all-consuming passion for growing vegetables. People everywhere are turning over their gardens to them and small allotments are at a premium. It could be said, however, that more interesting ways of actually preparing and cooking vegetables remain to be explored. While there is nothing nicer than a dish of plainly and perfectly cooked peas or spinach, there is no end to the many different ways of enjoying them and each and every vegetable under the sun.

The spread of vegetarianism has fortunately created new ways of looking at vegetables. No longer do we regard them as a limp afterthought, served with meat to fill up the plate; they are an important item in their own right and we have come to respect them very much as the people of the Far East and the Mediterranean have for centuries. This has led to more care and thought as to their preparation with a view to preserving their precious vitamins and minerals. They are also a valuable source of fibre, extremely low in calories and delicious to eat. Growing your own is therefore a logical progression, inspired as much by this renewed interest as by a desire to avoid unnecessary chemicals and fertilizers. It is still impossible, however, for the majority of us to grow vegetables but many a city window ledge or balcony could sustain a selection of fresh herbs which would greatly improve supermarket salads and vegetables. We can still concentrate on buying what is seasonal and freshest and maybe eat a few more, cutting down on high fat and chloresterol products in the process.

Colcannon

This is the traditional Irish dish of mashed potatoes and cabbage which was traditionally served, mixed with lucky charms, on Hallowe'en. Ireland produces lovely potatoes in many different varieties and good floury ones would be the right choice for this hearty dish. A piece of ham or bacon would go down well with this dish and is indeed the logical accompaniment though not essential.

To 2 cups of mashed potato add 4 cups of cooked shredded green cabbage or kale, 6 chopped spring onions (scallions) and 2 small leeks which have been briefly cooked in milk. Make sure the milky cooking liquid also goes into the potato together with a good knob of butter, salt and pepper and parsley. Mix well together until the mixture is well incorporated and is prettily speckled a delicate green. Any leftovers can be fried and enjoyed with a slice or two of bacon and a fried egg the following day.

'Did you ever eat colcannon
When t'was made with yellow cream
And the kale and praties blended
Like a picture in a dream?
Did you ever scoop a hole on top
To hold the melting lake
Of the clover-flavoured butter
Which your mother used to make?
Ah, God be with the happy days
When troubles we had not
And our mothers made colcannon
In the little skillet pot.'

Stanley Spencer (1891-1959) *Gardening*

7

Braised Fennel

Fennel is strongly assertive when eaten raw in salads and has a pronounced anise flavour. Cooked, it is a different vegetable altogether when it becomes sweet and mellow. I am, of course, talking about the bulb of the Florence fennel which is related to another type of fennel whose delicate leaves and seeds are also invaluable, especially with fish.

Allow 1 fennel bulb per person. Trim and reserve some of the outer leaves. Plunge the bulbs into boiling water and cook for about 20 minutes until tender but still firm. Drain well and when cool enough to handle, slice in half lengthways. Pile into an ovenproof dish, sprinkle with salt, pepper, olive oil and some coarse slivers of Parmesan cheese and bake in the oven for 15 minutes or so until brown.

Grey Mullet with Fennel

This would be a good way of cooking fish on an open barbecue when dry burning fennel twigs could be allowed to waft gently upwards and deliciously permeate the fish above. I should emphasize that only a very brief cooking time should be allowed using this method to avoid letting the fish dry out. Otherwise you could grill or broil the fish inside on the cooking stove.

Clean and scale 1 fish per person, leaving the heads intact and make several slashes across the body. Season well inside and out and place some lemon slices into the cuts and inside the fish together with a few fennel twigs. Lay more twigs in a fireproof dish and lay the fish on top brushing them with a good olive oil. Cook briefly under a very hot grill. The fish could be flamed in a little Pernod before serving to accentuate the anise-like flavour of the fennel.

Fennel seeds when soaked in wine
Revitalize a heart that love makes pine.

École de Salerne, 1500.

Victor Gabriel Gilbert (1847–1933) *The Square in front of Les Halles*

Courgettes (Zucchini) with Herbs

Courgettes are a versatile vegetable. They can be served as they are, in moussakas, salads, omelettes and tians and can be stuffed with all manner of interesting ingredients. As a bonus, their beautiful flowers can also be stuffed and deep-fried in a delicate batter to make fritters.

Coarsely grate up 2 lb (1 kg) courgettes, skins and all, and spread them out on a clean towel inside a colander to drain. Sprinkle with salt and leave for an hour or so. Squeeze the courgettes in the towel so that all the liquid runs out. Heat 3 tablespoons of olive oil, or a mixture of olive oil and butter in a pan and gently cook the courgettes until tender, turning occasionally. Sprinkle with lemon juice and fresh basil and parsley and serve immediately.

This mixture is very suitable for adding to a cooked omelette just before serving.

Walter F.I. Tyndale (1856-1943) *Miss Lydiard's Stall, Bath*

10

Pan Bagnat

Originally a peasant dish from around Nice in the South of France, this is a wonderful snack dish good for picnics and ideal for the beach when sea breezes whet the appetite. It traditionally contains flaked cooked tuna and a few salted anchovies, but a strict vegan or vegetarian could omit these.

You will need a very large crusty roll. Slice off a piece of the top and remove some of the soft centre. Cut a clove of garlic in half and rub the cut sides all around the inside. Fill with layers of sliced tomato, hard-boiled egg, a few olives, a few slices of cucumber and green pepper, a little chopped onion, the fish (optional), a few drops of vinegar, a tablespoon of olive oil, salt and pepper and a sprinkling of parsley. Put the top of the roll back on and wrap it tightly in plastic film leaving it in a cool place for the flavours to mingle.

Henry Maynell Rheam (1859-1920) *A Girl in a Garden by the Sea*

Beetroot Soup (Borscht)

This is the warming peasant dish of the Russian steppes. It can be made more hearty and sustantial by adding a little raw minced or ground beef but the flavour will not suffer greatly if you omit this.

Melt a little butter in a large saucepan. Sauté together 2 lb (1 kg) raw beets, which have been scraped and grated, 2 sticks of celery (diced), 3 chopped leeks, half a finely-shredded cabbage, 2 chopped onions and a clove of garlic. When the vegetables have started to go limp, add 3 pints (7½ cups) of water, a bouquet garni and a tablespoon of salt. Cover, and simmer for 2½ hours. Discard the bouquet garni. Just before serving, beat up the yolks of two eggs in ⅓ pint (1 cup) soured cream. Add a little of the hot soup to the mixture, then gently stir this into the soup taking care not to let it boil. A clear soup can be obtained by omitting this last stage and straining the soup when it can be served chilled. Garnish with a little cream and a sprinkling of chopped dill.

Beetroot is an unjustly neglected vegetable. Don't forget it can be cooked, grated and mixed with horseradish to make a tasty relish for fish, cubed in Red Flannel Hash, an American classic, served hot with butter or combined with oranges in a salad – what a colour combination!

Too many cooks spoil the broth.
Proverb

Italian School (15th century) *The Greengrocer* (fresco)

Lucas van Valkenborch (1530-1597) *Vegetable Market*

White Beans in Tomato Sauce

This is a traditional Greek dish and to be as near authentic as possible you could use large white beans such as butter beans or haricots. It is an excellent protein dish and a complete meal in itself, eaten perhaps with a little warm pitta bread to mop up the juices.

Beans are extremely versatile as well as nourishing. They are as delicious cold in salads, such as Tonno e Fagioli as they are hot in the famous Cassoulet of Carcassone: cold haricots verts are an important constituent of the Salade Niçoise of Southern France.

Soak the beans for about 4 hours or overnight. Fry chopped onion and a couple of cloves of garlic until translucent. Add some ripe tomatoes (canned are preferable to anaemic fresh ones), then the drained beans, a teaspoon of thyme or oregano and a few bay leaves. Barely cover with water and simmer until the beans are tender. Before serving, add a little lemon juice and sugar, some salt and pepper, and a little chopped parsley or coriander.

The way to a man's heart is through his stomach.
Proverb

15

Peas with Lettuce

This is a good way to improve the flavour of peas which may be past their first flush of youth. If there is no alternative but to use frozen ones, try to get the smallest, or petits pois type.

Take two hearts of lettuce and tuck some sprigs of fresh thyme or mint between their leaves. Put them in a pan with 1 lb (450 g) fresh hulled peas, a large knob of butter, a pinch of sugar, a little salt and half a glass of water. Bring to the boil and simmer for 15 minutes. Drain well and serve the vegetables hot.

Risi e Bisi

Rice is an important part of the cuisine of Northern Italy and a great deal of it is grown along the River Po in Lombardy. This is a way of cooking rice with peas invented by the Venetians.

Heat a couple of tablespoons of butter in a heavy pan and gently sauté some finely chopped onions and parsley. Add the peas (3 lb/1½ kg after shelling) turning them to allow them to absorb the fat. Cover with meat or vegetable stock, bringing them to the boil before adding 1 lb (450 g) rice. Cook without stirring until the rice is *al dente* but still moist like a *risotto*. Serve with extra butter and plenty of Parmesan cheese.

Sir Luke Fildes (1844-1927) *Dolly*

Garlic Broth Provençal

This is an unusual and wonderfully satisfying dish, especially if you love garlic as the French and Italians do. To 2½ pints (6 cups) boiling salted water add 6 or more crushed cloves of garlic, a sprig of sage and a bay leaf. Boil for 8 minutes more and remove from the heat. Beat 1 egg in a large bowl, then still beating, gradually strain the broth into the bowl. Add salt and black pepper to taste. Serve with fried French bread or croûtons.

John Bulloch Souter (ex.1914-1940) *Sorting Garlic*

Peace and happiness begin, geographically, where garlic is used in cooking.

Marcel Boulestin

Roasted Peppers

Something wonderful happens to sweet bell peppers when their skins are well charred before removing them. An easy way to do this is to stick a fork into the whole pepper and carefully turn it over the naked flame of your cooker until it has become evenly blackened. Place inside a plastic bag for a few minutes when you should find that the skins can be easily removed. Alternatively, roast them in the oven.

This dish makes an excellent starter and will look most attractive if you use an assortment of different coloured peppers. Prepare your peppers as described in the manner above, or in the case of a larger quantity, bake them whole in a fireproof dish placed inside a *bain marie* until the skins have darkened and wrinkled. Allow to cool, skin, and cut into long strips. Arrange on individual plates and cover the peppers with a dressing of olive oil and lemon juice with plenty of garlic and a few extra lemon slices.

Another way is to roast the peppers whole, stuffed with a whole peeled tomato inside each together with a little chopped garlic, 3 or 4 anchovies and a few chopped capers. Pour a little virgin olive oil over each or some of the oil in which the anchovies were packed. You will have no need to add extra salt to the peppers, the anchovies are quite salty enough.

Globe Artichokes

This intriguing vegetable can be prepared and eaten in a number of different ways. It can be stewed in a mixture of water and olive oil or boiled and served with garlic butter as a dipping sauce. The hearts alone are delicious in mixed hors d'oeuvres or with scrambled eggs as a light lunch dish. As a change, try them with this piquant sauce.

Trim the tough stalk and outer leaves from the artichokes. Cook in boiling salted water until each is tender at the base and an inner leaf can be easily pulled out. Leave to drain upside down. When cool enough to handle, remove the choke by gently opening up the centre leaves and carefully spooning it out. Close up the leaves again. For the dressing, take half a teaspoonful each of salt, black pepper, sugar and mix together with a teaspoon of French mustard until you have a smooth paste. Add 1 clove of garlic, peeled and crushed, 2 teaspoons crushed capers, 1 chopped gherkin (pickle) finely chopped, 2 shallots and 4 olives and some parsley, finely chopped. Add 6 tablespoons olive oil and 2 tablespoons wine vinegar. Mix well and use as a sauce in which to dip the succulent bases of the leaves and then the heart.

A. Raspal (1738–1811) *Provençal Cookery*

Ernest Masson (19th century) *The Potato Harvest*

Gratin Dauphinois

Perhaps the most versatile as well as the most widely used of all vegetables, this is a good potato dish to make when you are busy with other courses and is sufficiently glamorous to serve at a dinner party.

Peel and thinly slice 2lb (900 g) raw, waxy potatoes. Put them into a bowl and add pepper, salt, grated nutmeg, a beaten egg, 1 pint (2 cups) of scalded milk and ¼ lb (1 cup) Gruyère or other hard, grated cheese. Mix well together and put into an earthenware dish which has been rubbed with garlic and well buttered. Put a generous layer of cheese and a few nuts of butter on top and bake in a moderate oven for 45 minutes.

Potato and Watercress Soup

This is a most visually attractive soup. The taste and colour of the watercress comes through strongly as it is only very briefly cooked, thus retaining most of its nutrients.

Peel and cook 1 lb (450 g) potatoes in 1 pint (2 cups) of water or light stock and the same amount of milk. When cooked, place in a food processor and whizz until smooth. Reserve a few sprigs from a well washed bunch of watercress and add the rest to the potato mixture, processing briefly until it is finely chopped and thoroughly dispersed throughout the liquid. Gently re-heat before serving, seasoning well with a little salt and white pepper. Decorate with a few of the reserved watercress leaves.

An interviewer asked the Polish writer and
Nobel Prize winner,
Singer, whether he was a vegetarian for religious or health reasons.
'It is out of consideration for the chicken,' he replied.

Isaac Bashevis Singer (1904-)

Cabbage Soup

This is known as Garbure in France where classically it would contain bacon or slices of chorizo or other spicy pork sausage. It can, however, be just as nice without meat as can very many other dishes which have good amounts of vegetables among their ingredients.

Cut 1 small cabbage, 3 leeks, 1 carrot, 1 turnip, 1 onion and 2 sticks of celery and a clove of garlic into small pieces and sweat in butter until tender but not browned. Cover with 4 pints (2½ quarts) water, bring to the boil and season well. Add 2 potatoes, cut into large chunks, and a tin of haricot or other similar white beans. Simmer for one hour. The soup can be sieved or served as it is, whichever you prefer. In any case, croûtons of fried bread go very well with it and it makes a particularly robust winter meal.

Stuffed Cabbage

You will need a very large saucepan because the cabbage has to stand inside with the lid on. Different versions of this dish exist in many different countries, from Bulgaria and Germany to France and Russia.

Remove the damaged outer leaves of a large solid cabbage and carefully cut out a cavity in the centre, without allowing the rest of the cabbage to disintegrate. Carefully blanch with boiling water and leave to drain. Mix together 8 oz (1 cup) of minced or ground beef and the same amount of good quality sausage meat. Season well with salt and black pepper and press half of the mixture well down into the centre of the cabbage and the rest between the leaves. Tie the cabbage up with string to avoid it spreading during the cooking process. Melt 2 tablespoons of butter in the saucepan and sauté a chopped onion and carrot for a few minutes, then add 2 tablespoons of flour, blending it in carefully, and slowly add 1 pint (2 cups) stock or water. Put the cabbage in and tightly cover the saucepan. Bring back to a boil, then simmer gently for about 3 hours. Do not allow to dry out. If too much evaporation occurs, add a little more water from time to time. Remove the string and serve.

To make a good soup, the pot must only simmer or 'smile'.

French proverb

Michelangelo Caravaggio (1573–1610) *Still Life*

Cauliflower au Gratin

There is a powerful affinity between cauliflower and cheese as anyone who has sampled this popular dish would confirm. The same applies to broccoli. The dish can be made even more substantial by adding a few cooked farfalle or pasta shells in with the cauliflower before adding the sauce.

Break a large cauliflower up into flowerets and steam or cook in boiling, salted water until tender. In the meantime, make a well-flavoured sauce using Gruyère, Emmental, Cheddar or any similar type of cheese, together with a little Parmesan. Combine vegetable and sauce in an ovenware dish, sprinkle with more cheese and some breadcrumbs, which have been first fried in a little butter, and finish in a hot oven until the top looks appetizingly brown and bubbling.

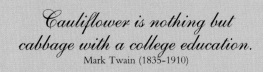

Cauliflower is nothing but cabbage with a college education.
Mark Twain (1835-1910)

24

Willem van Mieris (1662-1747) *The Greengrocer*

Glazed Carrots

This is a way of making new carrots even more delicious than they are already and gives them a 'dressed-up' look.

Scrape 1½ lb (700 g) young carrots and, leaving them whole, cook in boiling, salted water until tender. Drain off all but 2 tablespoons of the cooking liquid. Add 2 teaspoons of sugar and let it dissolve over a gentle heat. Add 4 tablespoons of butter and cook fast, shaking the pan to coat the carrots until the mixture has caramelized slightly. This technique can also be successfully applied to small onions or shallots and young turnips while they are still very small.

Small onions and baby mushrooms are glazed in this way and added to *Coq au Vin* in its final stage of cooking.

Eggs Crécy

Here is another way of using carrots, colourfully combined with eggs!

Leave 4 eggs to stand in boiling water for 5 minutes, remove, plunge into cold water and carefully peel. Scrape 1 lb (450 g) new carrots, cut into thin rounds and cook until tender. Make a cup of white sauce with 3 tablespoons of grated cheese and a little nutmeg, salt and pepper. Place the carrots in an ovenproof dish, lay the eggs on top and cover with the sauce. Sprinkle a little more cheese on top and brown in a hot oven.

Walter R.I. Tyndale (1856-1943) *At the Dose Venier*

25

Myles Birket Foster (1825–1899) *A Cottage Garden*

26

Beetroot Salad

This is a side dish well worth preparing if only for its wonderful colour. You must, however, start off with fresh young beets which you should trim and boil in salted water until tender.

Skin the beets, then slice and decorate them with finely chopped parsley and spring onions (scallions). Make a dressing of good olive oil and lemon juice seasoned with salt and pepper.
Another good way is to serve the sliced beets covered with a mixture of cream to which a little horseradish sauce has been added. This would go well with lightly battered and fried fish, also with a salad of cold roast beef.

Salade Niçoise

This may be a little too substantial to serve as a first course but would make a satisfying lunch dish. Rather than throwing all the ingredients into a salad bowl when the egg is bound to break up unattractively, it is better to arrange the salad on individual plates and hand the dressing round separately.

You will need a firm lettuce such as cos or romaine, 1 lb (450 g) cooked french beans, a few waxy, cooked potatoes, 3 or 4 hard-boiled eggs, 1 lb of ripe tomatoes, a can of tuna and a small can of anchovies. You could also add a few strips of green sweet pepper and some black olives. Cut up or slice all the ingredients as attractively as possible and arrange a little of each on individual plates. Serve with a well-flavoured, garlicky vinaigrette and a good sprinkling of chopped parsley or basil.

Spanish Omelette

One of these would make a substantial meal for two. You could even add slices of chorizo, chopped ham or bacon, cheese or vegetables, such as peppers or tomatoes. Small slices are served in Spanish tapas bars where, among a huge variety of other snacks, they are served with glasses of chilled sherry as part of a prolonged appetizer until dinner at 11 p.m or thereabouts.

Chop an onion and a clove of garlic and fry till golden. Peel and dice 1 lb (450 g) potatoes and add to the onion and garlic mixture. Slowly fry until tender but not crisp (you could use leftover boiled potatoes for this). Beat up 6 eggs with a few drops of water. Pour off any excess cooking oil from the pan then pour in the eggs.
When done on one side, turn over using a large plate to help you, and cook on the other side, using a little more oil if the pan seems dry. Serve immediately, but not rolled over – all Spanish omelettes are served flat.
The French *Omelette Parmentier* is not dissimilar. The omelette is not, however, turned over or served flat. Instead, small cubes of potatoes are first sautéed in butter, with perhaps a little chopped ham, and used as a filling for a classic 2- or 3-egg omelette.

Sir George Clausen (1852–1944) *The Allotment Garden*

29

Cucumber Salad

Cucumbers are delicate and cooling, equally delicious in thin sandwiches as they are in Greek tzatziki or Indian raita.

To slice cucumbers thinly you really need a *mandoline*. If you do not possess such an instrument you must do your best with a very sharp knife. It is up to you whether or not you first remove the outside skin. Perhaps you could compromise by removing half of it lengthways with a potato peeler which will result in an interesting striped effect when the cucumber is cut into rounds. You will need to remove any excess water from the vegetable, so when you have cut the cucumber as thinly as possible, sprinkle on a little salt and put into a colander with a plate pressed down on top. After a half hour or so, remove the cucumber, pat dry and dress with a few drops of olive oil and vinegar or lemon juice and garnish with chopped parsley or chives.

To make the best cucumber sandwiches, use the same method up to the point where the salted cucumber has been drained. Of course you must use as thinly sliced white bread as possible and good unsalted butter for the best results.

Tzatziki and raita are not dissimilar, both consisting of grated cucumber in a yogurt base, the former eaten with pitta bread or as a sauce and the latter with curries.

Joachim Bueckelaer (c.1530–1573) *The Vegetable Seller*

30

My salad days,
When I was green in judgement.

William Shakespeare (1564–1616) *Antony and Cleopatra*

Having ordered a pizza,
Berra was asked if he would like
it cut into four or eight pieces.
'Better make it four,' said Yogi,
'I don't think I can eat eight!'

Lawrence 'Yogi' Berra, U.S. baseball player

Stanhope Alexander Forbes (1857–1947) *The Onion Boy*

32

Onion Tart

In France, this is known as Pissaladière and is closely related to the Italian pizza.

For the base, a pizza dough is ideal, either bought ready-made or home-made. You could also substitute a flaky pastry base. This could be bought frozen, defrosted, and rolled out taking care to keep it cool at all times. If using pizza dough, keep to the traditional round shape. An oblong shape moulded to a baking sheet would look good for the pastry base. For the filling, gently fry $1^{1}/_{2}$ lbs (1 quart) of thinly sliced onions in a tablespoon of olive oil until they are translucent but not browned. Season to taste. Spread the onions evenly over the dough or pastry base and make a diamond pattern with anchovies over the entire surface. Place black olives in the centre of each diamond and bake at 375°F (190°C) for about 40 minutes. Serve hot, cut into slices.

French Onion Soup

This soup possesses a wonderful warming quality. In times past, porters at Les Halles, the former fruit and vegetable market of Paris, would have had an early morning bowlful of this to sustain them and keep them going in their heavy work of humping sacks of vegetables.

Peel and slice up 3 large onions and sauté them in a couple of tablespoons of butter until golden, then sprinkle with a little sugar so that they caramelize slightly. Add $1^{1}/_{2}$ pints (4 cups) of good beef stock or bouillon, bring to the boil and simmer for 20 minutes. Add a glass of white wine and salt and pepper and simmer for a further 10 minutes. In the meantime, toast 4 rounds of French bread. Place a slice each in 4 individual soup bowls, sprinkle grated Gruyère cheese on top then fill each bowl with the soup. Place the bowls under a hot grill until the cheese melts and bubbles. Serve immediately.

Leeks Vinaigrette

Leeks are sometimes called the poor man's asparagus, but served like this, in a warm salad, they have nothing to be ashamed about.

For four people, clean and slice lengthways 8 young leeks. Steam or cook them in boiling, salted water until the colour is bright and they are just tender. Meanwhile, stir together 2 teaspoons Dijon mustard, 1 tablespoon red or white wine vinegar and salt and pepper in a bowl together with the yolks of 2 hard-boiled eggs. Retain the whites. Stir until well amalgamated and perfectly smooth – the mixture should bear a passing resemblance to mayonnaise. Drain the leeks on kitchen paper and arrange on a pretty, heated oblong dish. Pour over the dressing and garnish with the chopped egg whites and parsley. Serve with warm whole wheat or white crusty bread.

Leeks make a excellent supper dish, trimmed, cooked and wrapped in slices of ham. Place in an ovenproof dish, cover with a rich cheese sauce and brown in a hot oven. Serve with a green salad and lots of fresh, crusty bread to mop up the sauce.

Let the salad-maker be a spendthrift for oil, a miser for vinegar, a statesman for salt, and a madman for mixing.
Spanish proverb

Camille Pissarro (1830–1903) *Vegetable Garden at the Hermitage, Pontoise*

Bubble and Squeak

This is an old-fashioned favourite for using up leftover boiled potatoes and cabbage or Brussels sprouts.

If you are starting from fresh ingredients, cook the
shredded cabbage first then add it to smoothly mashed potatoes.
Season well, then form into round cakes, dipping them in seasoned flour.
Fry in hot fat on both sides, remove and drain well on kitchen paper before serving.
This goes well with fried eggs and maybe some crisply grilled bacon slices for
non-vegetarians.

Swedish Cabbage and Apple Salad

This makes a welcome change from the ubiquitous cole slaw and is, I think, a good deal more interesting from the point of view of taste.

Wash 2 or 3 dessert apples very thoroughly as you are going to leave them unpeeled.
Grate them coarsely and mix them with 3 cups of shredded white cabbage. Mix
together with half a cup of double cream and the juice of an orange.
Serve slightly chilled.

Camille Pissarro *The Cabbage Slopes, Pontoise*, 1882

Imam Bayildi

This is one of Turkey's most beguiling dishes: the name means 'The Imam Swooned', which he no doubt did, with ecstasy, when confronted with this delicious dish of cold aubergines (eggplant).

Cut 6 medium-sized aubergines in half lengthways, sprinkle with salt and allow to drain for half an hour. Rinse and dry. For the stuffing, fry 1 lb (2 cups) chopped onions with 4 cloves of garlic until soft then add a thinly sliced pepper and 8 oz (1 cup) chopped tomatoes. Season well and cook gently until the liquid is somewhat reduced. Stir in some chopped parsley or coriander. Shallow fry the aubergines to seal and slightly brown them. Drain, make a slit in each half and fill with as much stuffing as possible. Place in a baking dish, open side up, garnish with tomato slices and almost cover the aubergines with tomato juice. Bake until tender – about 45 minutes. Allow to cool before serving.

George Bernard Shaw, the Irish writer and a staunch vegetarian, refused to attend a gala dinner because a wholly vegetarian menu was on offer. He said: 'The thought of two thousand people crunching celery at the same time horrified me.'

George Bernard Shaw (1856-1950)

Karl Frederick Nordstrom (1855-1923) *Garden in Grez*

38

Ratatouille

Richly evocative of the Mediterranean, this colourful vegetable stew is equally delicious hot or cold, on its own, or as a magnificent accompaniment to roast lamb.

There are many different combinations of vegetables that can be used but the most usual version can be made from 3 large aubergines (eggplants), 3 courgettes (zucchini), 3 sweet red peppers, 4 large ripe tomatoes, 2 cloves of garlic, two large onions, some coriander seeds and dried basil, though fresh would be better. Prepare the aubergines and courgettes by slicing them into rounds and putting them in a colander with a sprinkling of salt and a weighted plate on top. Leave for about an hour for the excess moisture to drain away. Meanwhile, prepare the other vegetables, skinning and chopping the tomatoes, slicing the onions and de-seeding and cutting the peppers into strips. Heat half a cup of good olive oil in a heavy pan, gently fry the onions and then the garlic until translucent but not brown. Add aubergines, courgettes, then peppers and tomatoes and a teaspoon each of coriander seeds and dried basil, if using. Add salt and pepper, cover and simmer gently for about an hour. Add torn basil leaves to finish.

Raoul Dufy (1877-1953) *The Market at Marseille*

Crudités

Raw vegetables make an excellent hors d'oeuvre, a great party dish, or even a light, healthy meal in their own right. They have always been a favourite of French bistros where they appear at the start of every menu, served in the form of piles of individual grated or matchstick vegetables – celeriac, carrots, beetroot – all tossed in a light and delicious mustardy vinaigrette.

This version consists of a mixture of raw, young vegetables – cauliflower florets, sweet peppers, tender peas in their pods, green beans, carrots, tomatoes, cucumber, celery, radishes, olives – whatever pleases you. Simply cut up into convenient pieces, leaving small vegetables whole, and arrange on a beautiful plate. Serve with dipping sauces of mayonnaise, aioli, rouille, tapénade (all of which can be bought ready-made) or concoct something delicious of your own.

Maximilien Luce (1858-1941) *La Rue des Abbesses*

Better is a dinner of herbs where love is than a fatted ox and hatred with it.

Proverbs 15, 7

Vichyssoise

This classic French soup makes a refreshing start to a summer meal and can be prepared well in advance. A variation of this could be made with fresh green peas instead of the leeks but would not be strictly authentic.

Put 1¹/₂ lb (700 g) cleaned chopped leeks, 2 chopped shallots and 2 small peeled potatoes into a heavy saucepan and allow them to gently sweat without browning for a few minutes. Add a mixture of water and white wine made up to about 1 pint (2 cups). Season well, bring to the boil and simmer for 20 minutes. Make a fine purée using a Mouli food mill or food processor. Mix in 1³/₄ pints (1 quart) milk. Cool down the soup and chill well in the refrigerator. Serve topped with a little fresh cream and some chopped chives. Serves 6.

George Barret the Younger (1767–1842) *Market Garden at Chelsea*

Greek Salad

This is almost a meal in itself and is strongly evocative of the Greek Islands and of lazy days spent in the sunshine.

You will need some crisp lettuce leaves, firm, juicy tomatoes, quartered, peeled and thickly sliced cucumber, onion rings, green peppers, cored, de-seeded and thinly sliced. Using the lettuce to form a base, pile up the other ingredients in layers aranging cubes of feta cheese and plump black olives on top. Sprinkle with fresh parsley, mint and marjoram. At a pinch, dried marjoram or oregano would do. Dress with two-thirds olive oil to one-third lemon juice, salt and freshly ground black pepper.

Stuffed Tomatoes

Make this dish when the huge beef tomatoes are available. They must be fully ripe but still firm enough to hold their filling.

Cut the tops off as many tomatoes as you need and remove the pips and some of the pulp from the centres using a spoon. Set aside to drain for a while. Meanwhile, make up a mixture of cold rice, chopped hard-boiled eggs, chopped fresh herbs, such as chives, chervil or parsley, and pepper and salt. Moisten the whole with a good quality mayonnaise and use the mixture to stuff the tomatoes. Replace their caps and decorate with more chopped parsley.
You can also make a cooked version of this dish where the rice is mixed with cooked minced beef or ham, a little garlic and minced onion and moistened with the pulp removed from the tomatoes. The tomatoes are then baked in the oven. Sweet peppers can be given exactly the same treatment.

Luis Menendez (or Melendez) (1716–1780) *Still Life with Tomatoes and Cucumbers*

Handed a salad at the table, Turner remarked to his neighbour: 'Nice cool green, that lettuce, isn't it? And the beetroot pretty red — not quite strong enough; and the mixture, delicate tint of yellow that. Add some mustard, and then you have one of my pictures.'

Joseph Mallord William Turner (1775–1851)

43

Carl Larsson (1853–1919) *Shelling Peas*

Green Pea Soup

A real winter warmer and a substantial meal in itself, the addition of a little ham or bacon stock would not go amiss but it is just as good without, making it an excellent choice for vegetarians.

Soak 8 oz (1 cup) split green peas overnight in cold water. The next day chop up 2 leeks and put them in a large saucepan with the drained peas, half a chopped lettuce, about 12 spinach leaves, a sprig of chervil, 3 tablespoons of butter, 4 teaspoons of sugar, some salt and 2 glasses of water. Bring to the boil, cover and simmer for about 60 minutes or until the peas are tender. Sieve, then add 2 pints (5 cups) lukewarm water, stirring with a wooden spoon. Bring to the boil and add a few more tablespoons of butter and 8 oz (1 cup) fresh cooked peas before serving.

Spinach Soup

This is popular in the Netherlands, made from the excellent produce of its market gardens and dairies.

Make a purée by cooking 1 lb (450 g) spinach in salted water and passing it through a sieve. Melt 2 tablespoons of butter, add a tablespoon of cornflour (cornstarch) and cook for a few minutes. Gradually add the spinach purée and then hot milk until you have the correct soup-like consistency. Season with salt and pepper and serve with croûtons and a little added cream.

Minestrone

You are unlikely to need any more to eat after a bowlful of this Italian classic soup.

You will need 3 lb (1½ kg) assorted vegetables – carrots, celery, cougettes (zucchini), cauliflower, potatoes, peas, leeks, onions, parsnips, marrow (squash), green beans – whatever you like. Clean and prepare them and cut them into similar-sized pieces. First, fry some chopped onion and garlic in olive oil until golden brown. Add the other vegetables and 3 pints (1½ quarts) water. Simmer for an hour then add a tin of chopped tomatoes and a tin of drained borlotti beans. Cook for another half hour or so until all the vegetables are tender. For an even more substantial soup a little cooked pasta could also be added. Serve garnished with fresh basil and grated Parmesan cheese.

    Pasta e Fagioli, (pasta and bean soup) bears a distinct resemblance to minestrone, at least from the point of view of taste. However, it contains fewer vegetables – tomatoes, onions, garlic, celery – enough to form the background stock in which the white beans and pasta are cooked.

Stuffed Mushrooms

For this dish you ideally need large, flat field mushrooms which have a natural hollow on their undersides in which to lay the stuffing.

Sauté a little finely chopped shallot or onion together with a clove or two of garlic. When cooked, make a stuffing by adding them to some white breadcrumbs, the chopped mushroom stalks and a generous amount of chopped parsley, pepper and salt and a drizzle of olive oil. Place the cleaned mushrooms upside-down on a baking tray, press the stuffing into the hollows formed by their gills and sprinkle more olive oil over. Bake in a hot oven for 8 minutes or so, or until the mushrooms are lightly cooked and the stuffing golden brown.

Frederick Richard Pickersgill (1820-1900) *Washing the Vegetables*

Imperial/Metric Conversion

Weights

2 oz	50 g
2½ oz	60 g
3 oz	75 g
4 oz	110 g
4½ oz	125 g
5 oz	150 g
6 oz	175 g
7 oz	200 g
8 oz	225 g
9 oz	250 g
10 oz	275 g
12 oz	350 g
1 lb	450 g
1½ lb	700 g
2 lb	900 g
3 lb	1.3 kg

Volume

5 fl oz (¼ pt)	150 ml
10 fl oz (½ pt)	275 ml
15 fl oz (¾ pt)	425 ml
1 pint	570 ml
1¼ pints	725 ml
1¾ pints	1 litre
2 pints	1.2 litres
2½ pints	1.5 litres
4 pints	2.25 litres

Index

Ernest Albert Chadwick (1876-1956) *Cottages at Broadway*